Conchas y Café Zine
Vol. VIII, Issue 3

Pen & Tongue
Pluma y Lengua

a  publication

DSTL Arts presents

Pen & Tongue / Pluma y Lengua

Conchas y Café Zine
Vol. VIII, Issue 3

Cover and Book Design: Luis Antonio Pichardo

ISBN: 978-1-946081-66-7

10 9 8 7 6 5 4 3 2 1

www.DSTLArts.org

Los Angeles, CA

Contents

fullstop

Mojdeh Amini

I digged the
backyard garden
buried all those words
Just close to that wise tree

The tree that its brain
has been swollen from
jargon words

nobody
can reach them
hear or read them

buried them deep
deep forever
if they grow

if they get roots
bury them again
deeper and deeper

Motkherasa*
(socrates's tv)
Gia Civerolo

Glowing red gems flicker

Crisp black log

Sparks break free

Eyes mirror flames

Memory mesmerize

Flames light cast spells

on hot summer nights

in ancient forests

Stories handed down

from the beginning of time

***Motkherasa**: Mesmerized by fire*
Etymology: "Moto" fire in Swahilli; "Hareerasayn" mesmerize
in Somali.

Zorro Sleeps

Abraham Jaramillo

Zorro sleeps seeking clouds so distant
serpents of light sounding savagely loud
obstruct and obliterate any hope for obvious passage
Zorro sends them a sentimental plea,
but sense is not a sentiment serpents can
comprehend and so they twist and bend,
they twist and bend
sorry... Zorro sleep time is up...!

Listen ("^") Up

Lois Jackson King

Bangity bangity bang
this chronic morning ring
I say what are they doing

squeaking and scraping
every morning no escaping
day after day after day

Rumble rumble rumble rumble
there goes shower pipes grumble
getting their morning ring too

Being on the lower floor
this is my morning chore
"Listen up" is what I do

A Message in Concept

T.D.M.

what were you dreaming

Gia Civerolo

Dawn drains deeply
night darkness

Pink light
paints picture
perfect pursed
lips lying

softly next to me
white sheets

sculpt the curves
of your bones

barely visible

beneath my

longing

lingering

gaze

Duplicandante

Luz Donis

No lo creo
Lo que veo
¿Eres tu?
¿O soy yo?

Había oído de ti
que podrías andar
por allí

Mi doble
aquí por fin
De plano la regué
¿En algo te avergoncé?

Conozco esa mirada
en nuestros ojos
dice
"¡Qué haces con tu vida!"
No sé en verdad

¿Y tú quien te crees?

Marissa

Marissa Cueva

I don't like the way they say my name.
Mah-rissah.
Mer-isuh.
Red, white, and blue,
threatening to bury my red, white, and green.

But it's Marissa,
the way my Tita says it.
The way my Tita sings it.
The way my Tita sighs it.
Soft A, sharp I,
whispering Ses.
Mari, Marisita,
Marissa.

Marissa
como el mar.
Di mi nombre
como olas pegando en la tierra
Y retirándose,
piedritas clicking against each other,
as the sea hisses away.

Marissa,
from Maria and Elisa.
De sus nombres viene el mio,
de sus vientres viene mi vida,
de sus sangres soy.

Marissa,
carrying with me Maria and Elisa,
and Guadalupe and Juan,
and Irma and Juan.
and Elvia and Juan.

8

¿Cómo ves, Marissa?

I am Marissa,
for Maria and Elisa,
and the things they could not do,
and the things they could not learn.
I am Marissa
for Lourdes who cleans the library,
and says "Qué bonito, qué bonito es
ser joven y estudiar.
¿Como ves, Marissa?"

Yo soy Marissa.
Marissa del Mar.
Marissa de Maria e Elisa.
Marissa con sangre jalisceña
Marissa que sueña en Aztlán.

Timeless Strength

Royal Roots

My people are royal, essential, brown and rich, like soil.
The deeper you go, the darker we grow.
Everyone knows;
The darker the berry, that's how it goes.
Royalty runs in our veins.
Ancient ways in the present days.
Wisdom that will always remain.
Learned to read the stars, created spiritual art,
Connected to Mother Earth with our heart.
Builders of sacred pyramids.
The world still marvels at what we did.

And Life Goes On

Lois Jackson King

La misma cosa
(the same thing)

President Lincoln
and Rev. Martin L. King
fought for the same thing
and both shot

Gettysburg Address
mm, mm, many are not kind
matching strong minds

gente de color
(people of color)

history Gray VS Blue
woo, woo, woo, it's true
now, it's Red vs Blue

the same separation today
"People of color" in dismay
all lives matter; march, march, "yeah"

color of Red is old "Gray"
people of color is still the prey
raw, raw, raw for those in blue

Ellos deben hacer más
(they must do more)

she tried

Gia Civerolo

She faces

Danger

Fear

Learning

No one

Believes you

Until you are

In a

Black

Body bag

No Soul

Sanjui

Amin! Amin!
Selu! Selu!
Afurrrr!
Clink!
Croth!
Crush! Crush!

Amin! Amin!
Sel! Sel!
Furrr!
Blin!
Arrggghhhh! Arrggghhhh!

Entre los Güeros

Luz Donis

Me siento bien
hueca, hasta los huesos
hueca como guacal
de ayote

No, sólo es una nigua
de bajo de mi huipil

Babosadas, es el antojo de un buen
aguacate o güisquil con espinas

Huehuecho!
Quisiera ser guacamaya
volando sobre un volcán
en Guatemala

Neudazallies*

Abraham Jaramillo

Cuando el estrés es difícil de soportar
y tu necesitas
un amigo para contar
de la forma en que fue el accidente automovilístico,
      de la chica de internet que conociste,
            del horrible y estresante trabajo que dejaste

Lo haremos
comeremos sushi en Little Tokyo o iremos al camión de tacos
por la noche
Lo haremos
beberemos boba 85° o vino 19 crímenes o cerveza 805

Sube el volumen,
"La Chica de Humo"
por Emmanuel está tocando
amigos, vamos,   Vamos…

---

*__Neudazallies__: la sensación de necesidad de salir con tus amigos. Etimología: del protogermánico *neudaz ("deseo, anhelo, ") y la palabra aliados (amigos). Además de pronunciar el final como "salir", que es salir en español.

Neudazallies*

Abraham Jaramillo

When the stress is hard to bear
and you need
a friend to tell
of the way the car accident went,
     of the girl from the internet you met,
        of the horrible and stressful job you left

We will
eat sushi at Little Tokyo or hit the late-night taco truck
we will
drink 85° boba or 19 crimes wine or 805 beer

Turn up the volume,
"La Chica de Humo"
by Emmanuel is on
friends, let's go,   Let's GO…

*__Neudazallies__: the feeling of needing to go out with your friends.
Etymology: from Proto-Germanic *neudaz ("wish, urge, desire,
longing") and the word allies (friends.) As well as sounding out
the end as "salir," which is "to go out" in Spanish._

Hay Unos Ojos

Marissa Cueva

Te quiero dedicar esta canción.
Como mi Abuelito le dedicaba a mi Tita,
como mi papá le dedico a mi mamá.
Esta te la dedico a ti.

Por esos ojos tan hondos,
que me pudiera perder en ellos.
Esos ojos tan intensos
que me paralizan.
Los ojos en cuales veo
una tristeza
que refleja la mía.

Por esos ojos
que han podido alcanzar
a mi tierna alma.
Que con una sola mirada,
traen paz,
y cada dolor se calma.

No puedo más que
adorarte
con cariño y dulzura.
Quererte
con frenesí y desesperación.

Te serenato con las canciones
de mis abuelos,
de mis padres.
De mi tierra,
de mi sangre.

Con trompetas que gritan con orgullo,
con violines que lloran con un gran pesar,

con las voces que han sobrevivido el tiempo,
con una pasión que nunca muere,
te dedico esta canción.

Perduembrace*

Royal Roots

Oblivious to time and reality.
The world disappears around me.

All I can do is surrender,
breathe you in,
feel your heartbeat.

Your aura is mesmerizing.
Your caress, timeless.

*Etymology: French word for lost is "perdu" and embrace... The
feeling of being lost in a hug

Yours Alone

Lois Jackson King

Dote suma dote suma
Darling dear darling dear

Toto gi ma toto gi ma
please always be mine

Kuo bafoo togante
we belong together

Piyo dora subarate
always and forever

Nando pa huff pilla
Nightly I long for you

Quri su epuco nunlia
Waiting for your lips

Hofkrigioa[*]
(50,000 thoughts a day is the human way)
Gia Civerolo

Suffocating heat
Dripping sweat melts
into white tangled sheets

Where

I keep stolen moments
Turning them into silk

Suspending art objects
8 sided
in my twisted web

Trapping thoughts
of you
Day and Night

8 spider legs
refuse to let go
even when you
beg "Pretty please"

Hofkrigio: When you can't get something or someone out of
your head.
Etymology: "Hoofd krijgt"–something and head in Dutch;
"Gio" Italian for boy.

I Loved You

Marissa Cueva

I loved you.
I loved you for the way
your eyebrow furrowed,
feigning anger.
I loved you for the way
your eyes shone,
as you looked at me.
I loved you for the way
you smiled at me,
an adorable lopsided smirk.

I loved you for the way
you shaped your fingers into a heart
over a FaceTime call.
I loved your voice,
I loved your hands,
I loved your soft curls between my fingers.

I loved that each time I saw you
my heart would swell,
and my mind would race
with a hundred stanzas
for a dozen poems.

But 'I love you'
began to sound more like a plea.

Born
from dark nights
on your parent's couch.
From nose kisses,
and cheek pinches,
and butt squeezes,
and holding hands by the pinky.

It died
in nights spent
screaming it
on the floor of my backyard,
on the phone with my mother,
crying in my best friends' arms.

By then
it was less the romantic whisper,
and more a desperate plea.
I love you.
I love you.
I loved you.

The Moon

Mojdeh Amini

It has been for a while
since moon has gone missing

I told the stars about it
they had no idea
what to do about it
It was pointless
to tell sun about it

Since then
night comes only
with its darkness
knocking on my
window
up to ceiling
Moon is the only one
can light up

To be up there even
When it's half or less

When night comes
And brings

It has been for a while
since moon has gone missing

I have a window
It's a tall window
tall up to ceiling

Up to sky
It's my eye
my window
to the sky

Vacancy

Gia Civerolo

tin tin por la cabeza

River

e l c e r e b r o
onomatopéyico

      umbrales
      umbrellas
      umbraguas
      celestes

peyico pico pico
rico, pico pieces

           chirrido
           cher u bs
           chirp chirp
           quer u bines

        esperan las jaulas
        dendríticos y fallas

fractales   alfombroso
        ositos con alas
        aguas sin almas

 s wa llo ws y pa u sa s

rin rin, motas se llaman
clic clic, fotones susurran

ou ou,
la quietud se enrosca
         se enrolla
       se enreda
      ¡pin pin!
brillantina recuerda, las
           fotos amadas

ting ting in the head

River

t h e b r a i n
onomatopeic

>   threshholds
>   paraguas
>   holdbrellas
>   celestials

cheepeep beak beak
peak, pecker pieces

>   chirp chirp
>   quer u bines
>   chirrido
>   cher u bs

>   they wait for cages
>   dendrites and faults

carpet   fractals
>   little winged bears
>   soulless waters

tragagolo ndr inas y p a use s

ring ring, motes call
click click, photos whisper

oh, oh
the quiet curls up
>   rolls up
>   tangles up
>   ping ping!
glitter remember,
>   beloved pictures

In and Out

Mojdeh Amini

In and out of
lights and
darkness

darkness
and lights
come to us

when we are low
when we are high

But do we know them?
But do we see them?
But do we read them?

lights and
darkness
meet   pass us

But do we know them?
But do we see them?
But do we read them?

In and out of
ourselves and
Ourselves

en los meses a dentro de la luz de la cocina después la concusión se torno traidor la luz y el cerebro de mi hija

River

blic
   blic
la luz
flickers

blink - blink - blink
ella me dice
"me duele, mommy"

blink blink

"me duele, mommy"

sus ojos puntos de pabilos
¡pu ¡pu
su cerebro conmocionado
pa! pa!
concusión
…pikaà sussussss pikaà…

cortocircuitos
            |
     c r a c k l ekill
       cortafuegos
   rayas a raya subrayan
        yo
          corto circuitos

tap tap tips tap
los dedos dicen con silencio
  no puedo oirlo
la moción más que
waves shaking air
sheka shika shika
blic blic

cortocircuitos
¡parpardeame!
déjala, maldit
dit
ditdit
ditos
        shhhhhh
golpes fotones

ziep— electrón mortal
be gone cuarcs
lo grito

pah! pah!
success on lips
        me me
          su su

          la luz
        mi mi
        sh sh

        mommy
        ma mi

fantasmas sssss   en los cables
        ahuyente ahuyente
no puedo disculparlos

in the months inside the kitchen light after the concussion turned traitor my daughter's brain and light

River

blink
  blink
the light
parpadea

par - par - par-
She says
"it hurts, mami"

 bleec bleec

"it hurts, mami"

 her eyes, candle wick points
!pu !pu
her shaken brain
pa! pa!
concussion
...peekkaa sussussss peekkaa...

 short circuits
               yo
      c r e p i tamato
       firebreaks
rayas a raya subrayan
           I
      short circuits

tap tap tips tap
fingers silently say
    i can't hear
the motion more than
ondas temblando el aire
shaka sheeka sheeka
bleeck bleeck

short circuits
blink me!
leave her, you bad
bad
badbad
little things
            shhhhhh
photon whacks

ziep—deathly electrons
llevase quarks
I shout

pah! pah!
éxitos en labios
            me me
            hers hers

            the light
            my my

            sh sh

            mami
            mah mee

ghostss hisssss in the wires
            out   out
I cannot forgive them

Hospital Language

Marissa Cueva

I know
the names of all of the medications
that my grandmother takes.
I know
the names of all of the treatments
that my brother received.
I know
the effects of every organ failure
that took my grandfather from me.

By eighteen,
I knew that my grandmother takes her pills
at 8:00 pm every night.
I knew that she's broken her right wrist,
right arm, left elbow,
and femur,
and dislocated her left shoulder.
I knew she took anti-inflammatory pills
for the pain in her knee
and antidepressants
after my grandfather passed.
I knew that she walks after she eats
to make up for her missing gallbladder.

By twelve,
I knew that my grandfather
had a triple-bypass open heart surgery,
which resulted in
liquid in his lungs,
and eventually kidney failure.
I knew that he had to have his lungs drained,
and have dialysis weekly.
I knew that the hospital cafeteria

had menudo on Sundays,
and chili on Thursdays.
I sat in waiting rooms as a little girl
and learned what each of the color codes meant.

Code Blue in room 463.
Code Blue in room 234.
Code Blue in room 351.
Code Blue Guadalupe Franco.

By eight,
I knew what a Rhabdomyosarcoma tumor does
to the body of a three-year-old little boy.
I knew what chemo, and radiation,
and surgeries, and blood transfusions
and hospital visits, and isolation,
do to the spirit
of a boy who was much too young,
much too innocent,
for all of it.

Growing up visiting the people I love
in hospitals
and at cemeteries,
this language is not unfamiliar to me.
The language of doctors,
the language of nurses,
the language that induces
anxiety and suspense
and indescribable fear.

Tainted Blood

Sanjui

Tink, tink, tink
Bleep, bleep, bleep
Incessant progression
From what it was
Dripping into the heart,
Giving life, candidly.

Glush, glush, glush
Gurgle, gurgle, gurgle
Dreaded encounter
To where it is now,
Dripping into the heart
Draining life, deceitfully.

Nonstop. Poisoning. Limiting.

Words and Sounds

Lois Jackson King

Craziness, all of this bemm bemm roogga
wondering what's with my body; much cooga cooga
Still with a sound mind, it says, "You go, girl"
but the body, says, "Yeah, right; I'll catch up later"
Anxiety of what I'm going through is much greater
One moment the body is at ease, then wowe
Ding-ong-it I'm trying my best to adjust, I want to
alleviate this excruciating pain but no physical a-toning
nights of hoos; moaning and much groaning
I tell myself, go to sleep, try and rest; do I listen
this is only temporary; great; I cry out cogua-mugga
Where is my faith; I will come through, this I pray
For spiritual peace, I sing, "Pain, pain, please go away"
Please please, do not come back to me, no other day
Many creaking utterances from my mouth; shoo-tittle
hoo-yie, I know help is on the way; I will not pout
Continuing sounds of my bones sounding out
Both days and nights with a heavy shout
mighty pain in knees, squeaking, speaking to me
My body sounds; giving off signals and such
Doctors say, "Age is known to usher in joint issues"
News update, I met joint issues at the age of twelve
I'm in good health; praise God; but the joints are on strike
With prescriptions, and with lessons of therapy, I'll be alright

Hobo Brother and Son

Gia Civerolo

La llegada

Saint Francis Hospital 9:10pm

Luz Donis

Tik tok   tik tok   tik tok   tik tok   you don't stop

whapa whapa whapa whapa whapa whapa ... allí estás

drip   drip   drip   en ti me enfocaré
drip   drip   drip   no te soltaré

wowowowowowowowowowow
swishhhswoosh swooshhh
posiciónate

Mmmmm   mmmmm   mmmmmm
....   whoooooooooo
....   whoooooooooo

tik tok   tik tok   tik tok   tik tok
drip   drip   drip   drip

Uuuuuuh   Uuuuuuuuuh   mmmmmmmm
¿Cuánto tiempo más?

Tik tok drip Tic tok drip Tic tok drip
AAHH   AAHH   OOOH OOOH
Sé que vales la pena

Tiktokdrip Tiktokdrip Tiktokdrip
UGH! UGH! UGHHHHHH!!!
HEE HEE! HOO HOO!

AAAAGGGHHH!!!!!
SQUISH   SWOOOOSH
GUSHHHH
slurp slurp

Pat Pat Pat Pat

Wuah!   WUAH! W U A A A HHH!
Snip   CLANGclip

Ven a mis brazos

Blabla-bla

Abraham Jaramillo

Tucku ku kurururu!
Meee Miiii-Hiii
Bada-bin Bada-ra-raa!
Chibi biki riky
Turun Turun TUN plung…

Oh Wonder

T.D.M.

Curious comes small.
Watcher and Eaters feeding
off Rainbows of grass.

Watch Your Step

Lois Jackson King

Whoa there, watch your step, squish squish
Oh look out, oh my, it's too late
You're stepping in the dog's food plate
Now he is licking all over your shoe
Squeaking and tracking food all across the floor
Clink clink; that's right please continue out the door
A little laughter will keep you from being blue
Whatever with your new shoes will you choose to do
We all make some kind of mistakes
Just look back and give yourself a break
Don't beat yourself up or hide your face
Think first; then take your place; run at your pace

Kaijufun*

T.D.M

Sniff, sniff, a blissful whiff

A downstairs so clean in sparkles, so shiny

Upstairs to the room for a quick shower

Did I make sure to pick up everything I need before?

Ahhhh so nice so clean and ready for just about anything!

Downstairs I go… beholden my eyes unknown.

The eating table a magical mess, whose surface in such stress?

Sofa adorned with food, papers, and knickknacks in a playful sprawl,

spots of brown, and greys, a whimsical sight, where chaos befalls.

What could have led to such muck?

So much destruction with heart palpitations

Reminds me of a place that reads "under construction".

Rawr or rawr I feel like a big Monster ran through the place

creating a realm of chaos, where nothing remains commonplace.

"Yua dah dah dah dah," splitter & splatter, in comes the first Kaiju,

"We yuuu we yuu wee yuu, who hoo!" in comes the second Kaiju,

"De doo de doo," with a razzle-dazzle, in comes the third Kaiju.

Oh, now I see it's the three little Kaijus in front of me,

Two nieces and a nephew all aflutter, as I stand in awe, quizzically.

No more no more Tanoshi, says I with laughter, when I was
　　　　face-planting and crying inside,

they brought joy thereafter.

***Kaijufun** (kai-joo-fun): A fun and entertaining manifestation of persons or events leading to the whimsical creation of a new state from chaos. For example, spiritual chaos when kids are unleashed on something.
Etymology: "Kaiju" (怪獣), referring to giant monsters like Godzilla, and "fun," representing the notion of enjoyment and playfulness embodying excitement. Japanese word plus fun*

*** So Tanoshi in Japanese "tanoshii 楽しい" means pleasant, delightful, enjoyable, or fun!

I left it out in my fictitious word because it sounded more like a name in the verse.

the pretty house

Mojdeh Amini

the walls of
   the pretty house

are getting swollen
   it's swallowing   all
   the smiles   all
   the laughters   in   any rhythms

the stairs of
the pretty madhouse

are shutting down
   cutting down   all
   the music   all
the songs   with   no rhythms

the windows of
the pretty dark house

are climbing to the sky
   shining on   all
   cracking classes   all
the bones hidden   indoors

Painted Desert Motel

Gia Civerolo

Bramanassa
(Of Pure Life)
Luz Donis

Sumantu! Anatimani e santo jana
Listen! Humble and peaceful people

Esa le maggo
This is the path

Pa ye purisattame
For an excellent man

Bhavatu sada satima
Become always mindful

Satim vata anicca
Aware of impermanence

Bhavatu sampanno
Become wise

Munica dukkhassa
Let go of all suffering

Desesi mettam me sabbattha
Learn love for everyone

Uncertain, Happy

Sanjui

Wagon ride, 1970's.
Valadeces, Mexico.
Sweet summer, our time.
Penetrating, Pungent odor,
Opening up our nostrils
Hitting the insides
From a mule and a yegua's manure,
My Guelo's coolest companions.

Wobble Wobble as they pull guelo, guela, my sisters,
And me on his transportation mode–el Guayín–
Dry all over, wood thirsting a drink of paint,
a splash of water,
Or maybe more rides.
With odd shaped wheels
Shaking from side to side,
Mere incoordination between
The companions and el Guayin.

Then piercing, exquisite smells
Travel in our direction
As we move on our journey
To comb the cornfields
And retrieve their gold,
The corn stalks for our next meal,
Tortillas de maíz
And for dessert, mouth-watering elotes con chile.

Wagon rides, yucky manure, enticing elotes

Where happiness was found at every turning corner,
Certainly.

Road Signs

Gia Civerolo

Taste and See

Lois Jackson King

I know there is no place like "our home"
With my(meow) cat, my siblings, I'm never alone
Pleasures of the day always fill our space throughout
Mm, mm the aroma I smell makes me run and shout
Should I tell everyone what it's all about
Noises "Cling-Clang, Bang" plus the smell
I know it's from the kitchen; oops, tumbling on the dog's pail
Veo a madre y abuela (I see mother and grandmother)
On the stove (en la estufa), "Chili" in a large pot
The pot is singing "bulp bulp bulp" and it's piping hot
On the table, (Mesa de comida, Queso rallado, tomates
        cortados) chips
Refried beans, avocados, shredded cheese, diced tomatoes, dips
Hot smell of the peppers; onions and beautiful whipped sour cream
Bowl and plate had plenty a blessed feast; this is so supreme

Gracias mama, gracias abuela
(thank you mama, thank you grandma)

Spotty Spoons

T.D.M

Sprinkle, spackle, speckle spitting spotting spoons.
Ruminates a room in merry.
oh full of sprinkles dancing around lights
oh spread of spackle holding the holes with might
oh dotted of speckles the floor resonates with color
oh wet of water the spitting commences over yonder
oh seen of spotting the troublemakers running in glee
oh target of the spoons speeding away merrily.
Now caught are the spoons, spotted, spitted, speckled, spackled
      and sprinkled.
So, sprinkle, spackle, speckle spitting goes spotting spoons
      never after.

Fin

Coffee Ice Beer

Gia Civerolo

Summer Reading Challenge

Alayna Abravanel

As you may know, the Summer Reading Challenge is next week and I will read for 20 minutes each day, and everyday, and get a prize for signing up for the Summer Reading Challenge. My question to you is, how long does it take for you to finish your books and return them, and get a new one? And the other question is, do you bring your laptop to the library to check out books from Libby and buy books on my birthday on July 29th at the library book sale used books?!

What is Summer Reading Challenge? Well, basically it is like when you read an article and use your imagination. What you should or should not do, like talking loudly and drinking at the library, when you know you are not supposed to do it. Why did you do it when you know you're going to be kicked out of the library, and getting kicked out from the library is not a privilege? By telling them what to do and when it comes to summer @ Etta, then I will enjoy myself there and go to different places, like the library and take notes on my iPad 8th generation.

Your Words

Marissa Cueva

I hate that it's your voice in my mind
that I hear when I begin to feel insecure.
"My girl is beautiful," you said,
the two of us in our underwear,
in my kitchen.
You pulled me closer to you,
gently moving my arms
which I had wrapped around my midsection,
so that you could admire me.
Your hands and your eyes
graced every insecurity.

But I'm not your girl anymore.
And my arms remain wrapped around myself,
as I stand,
naked and alone
in front of the mirror.

He said he liked my poetry.
He let me read it to him,
my small tears dampening his shoulder.
He said he liked my Spanish.
He'd pull my face close to his,
asking me to repeat the words,
his eyes staring intently,
while I whispered to him.
He said he liked my voice.
He said he liked my body.
And he kissed and loved every piece of me.

He said he liked that we had similar values.
He said he liked the way that I danced
and the way that I moved.
He watched with wide eyes

as I spun and swayed my hips,
to music unfamiliar to him,
the colored lights reflecting off my skin.
He liked to give me hickeys
where no one could see them.
He liked to kiss me at red lights
until the cars behind us honked.
Now I have to learn to like myself
without your eyes and your words.

"I'm not going anywhere," you told me.
"I want to work on things," you said.
"I love everything about you. I love you."
Which words did you mean,
if not those?

mermaids cry too

Gia Civerolo

The sound of blue
wetness crashes
across my body

A tiny tan crab's
skeleton slips silently
through sand
same tan color

No one registers its existence

The lonely black crow
seems out of place, caws
mysteries of the world

I could not decipher

Seagulls sonic sound
tries to block the sun
streaming bright day stars
sparkles on mirrored water

Sunset splashes colors
painters wish they knew

Cacophony of waves
orchestrates their death
and their birth
all at the same time

Over and over again

Pink rose petals swirl
white foam curls
around my
purple painted toes

Sacrifices

memories of you

i'm a

Mojdeh Amini

i'm a
bird in a cage
fish in a bowl

i'm a
lion in a zoo
horse in a street

i'm a
forest in a vase
ocean in a cup

i'm a
woman in a box
man in a tear

i'm a

Lost in Bliss

Royal Roots

Landscape crowned in
Majestic evergreen.
Aromatic resins take over.
Crisp cleanliness fills the air.

Sweet sounds of peace;
Birds whistling,
Leaves rustling,
Cascades murmuring,
Age-old songs from Source.

Cold wet bodies find warmth
Nestled into curves of ancient giants.
Ancestors eroding.
Meandering down the rapids,
Flowing down the streams.

Hyggrebi*

Michelle Smith

I miss his essence.
It is fleeting in leaves
that grow in all seasons
glow in all colors
and blow in the wind.
A beckoning on my shoulder
a perched watchful wise owl in a tree.
Am I dreaming of komorebi?
Your warmth of your spirit
bakes the rustling fronds on the ground.
With my every step
their crunchiness
speaks to your essential sturdy spines.
The stillness is
a misty watercolor memory;
a fleeting moment that I wish
could be reality.

***Hyggelig**: Danish and Norwegian. It means for mood of coziness
with feelings of wellness and contentment.
Komorebi: Japanese. It means the sunlight that filters through
the trees.

Tiempo

Sanjui

Serena, simpática soñadora
Solía sonreír sútilmente
Para silenciar su inapacible alma,
Pensando entre sollozos en su causa.

Intentó tanto tiempo tapar sus heridas
Y no tanto tardó que al aire todo salió.
Ya sin este terrible dolor, otro camino tomó.

Atravesó el bosque de sus temores y suspiró.
Serena, segura, sin titubeos, sonreía hacía el sol.

El tiempo lo permitió.

The Final Week of Conchas y Café

Alayna Abravanel

How do you say goodbye in Spanish? Saying goodbye is to LOL with the teachers and the incredible staff who have helped me.

Writing Time
(Joy of My Past)
Lois Jackson King

Cock-a-Doodle-do
up up all of you

Peck peck peck peck
chickens with their beak

squeak! Haw-man poop
my shoe is now a scoop

flap flap flap hurry away
Get over there, you, and stay

Buk buk buk ba-gawk
hens laying many eggs

Clap clap clap wonderful
Having chickens is meaningful

About the Authors
.... Sobre los autores

Mojdeh Amini

As a bilingual, Mojdeh enjoys and loves writing poems and prose in English.

Gia Civerolo

Gia Civerolo is a LA poet. She is publishing her first full-length collection *She Confuses Lovers, Movies, Angels & Poems*. She has published in *Spectrum*, *Four Feather Press* and is featured in the *Bards of Southern California: Top 30 SoCal Poets*. She can be seen at LA open mics.

Abraham Jaramillo

Planet Earth Artist, bound to create art that reflects nature, a range of human emotions, and a multitude of other topics using different types of media, such as poetry, photography, painting, etc. To discover more of his madness, follow him on his Instagram (@abraham_photoworld), or his website www.a0jphotoworld.com.

Lois Jackson King

A retired educator with degrees in Social Behavior, Christian Education and Christian Counseling as well as an Ordained Minister of the Gospel. Mother of 4, a grandmother of 10, a great-grandmother of 11, and one great-great-granddaughter.

T.D.M.

A debut author with a passion for creating human experiences. T.D.M. is a lifelong designer, creator and photographer exploring all forms of creative expression hoping to make a positive impact in the world.

Luz Donis

Luz is a second generation Guatemalan, raised in Boyle Heights. She trained and worked as a nurse for L.A. County and L.A. Unified. She is currently immersed in Vipassana insight meditation, ceramics, and being a grandma.

Marissa Cueva

Marissa Cueva is a 19-year-old Mexican-American student at Loyola Marymount University. She is a third-year Screenwriting major and a Chicano/Latino Studies minor. She pursuing a career in writing for the film industry and also has a prominent interest in writing poetry and other forms of prose.

Royal Roots

Royal Roots is a multidisciplinary artist based in Los Angeles. Her creations focus on uplifting her Afro-Indigenous roots in Mexico and El Salvador and the importance of reconnecting with nature. She believes we are all creators, and our art is a gift to heal the world. www.instagram.com/yourroyalroots

Sanjui

Sanjui is an educator, mother of 4 adult kids. She loves to read and write, and loves spending time with family. You can find her at favorite places, which are the beach, the library, and the park.

River

A River le gusta jugar con palabras y forma, y escribe principalmente en ingles pero disfruta escribir en español/ASLWrite, y raramente en otros idiomas. River likes to play with words and form. They write mainly in English but enjoy writing in Spanish/ASLWrite, and on rare occasion in other languages. www.chillsubs.com/user/River

Alayna Abravanel

Alayna Abravanel joined our Conchas y Café workshop series after participating in our *Journal of My Life* series offered in partnership with the Los Angeles Public Library. Alayna tries to express herself in as many was as she can.

Michelle Smith

This Vintage Tigress prowls and pounces from Los Angeles. Since 2017, my poems have grown tree branches that extend leaves of love, and bear fruit for the soul. My creative writings and photos are published by DSTL Arts, *Four Feathers Press*, *Spectrum*, & the Los Angeles Poet Society. Gracias DSTL Arts.

About the Conchas y Café program

Conchas y Café is a 12-week workshop series for adults, focusing exclusively on creative writing, literacy, and illustration. Participants have the opportunity to work with volunteer writers and artists on developing artwork that will be published and presented in a triannual 'zine and public reading.

For more information, locations, and dates for upcoming Conchas y Café workshops, contact us by email at *info@DSTLArts.org*.

Acerca el programa Conchas y Café

Conchas y Café es un taller de 12 semanas para adultos, especializando en escritura, literatura, y dibujo. Participantes tienen la oportunidad de trabajar con escritores y artistas voluntarios en el desarrollo de obras de arte que serán publicados y presentados en publicaciones trimestrales y lecturas públicas.

Para más información, localidades, y fechas de próximos talleres de Conchas y Café, contáctenos por correo electronico al *info@DSTLArts.org*.

This program is supported in part by:

See My Words: Conchas y Café Zine; Vol. 8, Issue 1
available now at **DSTLArts.org/shop**

Conchas y Café Zine
Vol. VIII, Issue 2

Estran gulados

a DSTL arts publication

Estrangulados: Conchas y Café Zine; Vol. 8, Issue 2
available now at DSTLArts.org/shop

This publication was produced by DSTL Arts.

DSTL Arts is a nonprofit arts mentorship organization that inspires, teaches, and hires emerging artists from underserved communities.

To learn more about DSTL Arts, visit online at:
DSTLArts.org
@DSTLArts